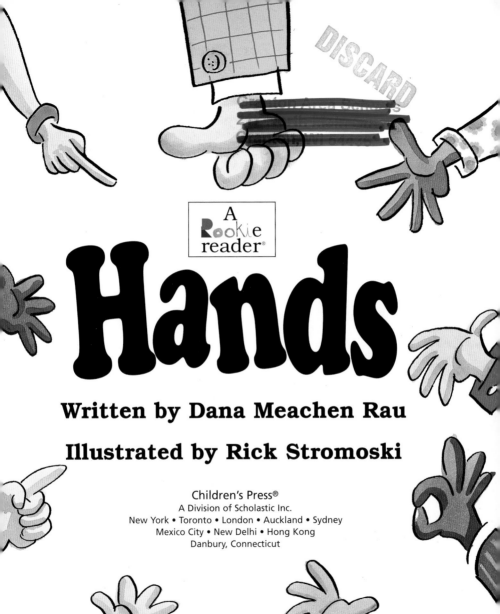

A Rookie reader®

Hands

Written by Dana Meachen Rau

Illustrated by Rick Stromoski

Children's Press®
A Division of Scholastic Inc.
New York • Toronto • London • Auckland • Sydney
Mexico City • New Delhi • Hong Kong
Danbury, Connecticut

For Charlie
—D.M.R.

For Molly and Danna
—R.S.

Reading Consultants
Linda Cornwell
Coordinator of School Quality and Professional Improvement
(Indiana State Teachers Association)

Katharine A. Kane
Education Consultant
(Retired, San Diego County Office of Education
and San Diego State University)

Library of Congress Cataloging-in-Publication Data
Rau, Dana Meachen.
    Hands / by Dana Meachen Rau; illustrated by Rick Stromoski.
    p. cm. — (Rookie reader)
    Summary: Children use their hands for all kinds of things when they prepare for
and go to a birthday party.
    ISBN 0-516-22009-8 (lib.bdg.)   0-516-27043-5 (pbk.)
    [1. Hand Fiction. 2. Parties Fiction. 3. Birthdays Fiction. 4. Stories in rhyme.]
I. Stromoski, Rick, ill. II. Title. III. Series.
PZ8.3.R232Han 2000
[E]—dc21   99-15865
                                                                              CIP

© 2000 by Children's Press®, a Division of Scholastic Library Publishing
Illustrations © 2000 by Rick Stromoski
Printed in China.
10 R 09   62

Hands.

5

Hands can buy.

Hands can bake.

9

Hands can tie.

11

Hands can make.

Hands say "Hi!"

15

Hands can clap.

Hands untie.

Hands unwrap.

21

Hands.

Word List (11 words)

bake
buy
can
clap
hands
hi

make
say
tie
untie
unwrap

About the Author

Dana Meachen Rau is the author of many books for children, including historical fiction, storybooks, biographies, and early readers. She has written *A Box Can Be Many Things*, *Purple Is Best*, *Circle City*, and *Bob's Vacation* (which she also illustrated) in the Rookie Reader series. Dana also works as a children's book editor and lives with her husband, Chris, and son, Charlie, in Farmington, Connecticut.

About the Illustrator

Rick Stromoski is an award-winning humorous illustrator whose work has appeared in magazines, newspapers, children's books, advertising, and network television. He lives in Suffield, Connecticut, with his wife, Danna, and five-year-old daughter, Molly.